CU00663188

&
Northumberland

Zymurgy Publishing, 2005

The moral right of Martin Ellis, the

author has been asserted.

A CIP catalogue record for this book is available
from the British library.
Cover design Nick Ridley
Printed & bound in Great Britain by
William Clowes Ltd, Beccles, Suffolk
ISBN 1 903506 16 6
Published by Zymurgy Publishing,
Newcastle upon Tyne
1 0 9 8 7 6 5 4 3 2

The Little Book of Tyneside and Northumberland is a capsule book for those too pushed for time or energy to read *A Tyneside and Northumberland Miscellany*. It aims to entertain and inform.

Sheep V People

t is estimated that there are five times as many sheep as people living in Northumberland.

Where Did The Term Geordie Come From?

No one knows for certain where the term Geordie comes from, the following are possible explanations.

Locally the term is used to describe someone from Tyneside, throughout Britain and the world it used to describe someone from the north-east.

First Suggestion

During the 1745 Jacobite Rebellion Newcastle was bypassed by the Jacobites, as it was a securely guarded garrison that supported King George. It was said that the region was all "for George" - leading to the name 'Geordie' derived from George.

Second Suggestion

The Oxford English Dictionary states that the word was first used in 1876 to describe miners/pitmen. Perhaps the name originated from the region's coal mines.

Third Suggestion

George Stephenson's miner's lamp was used by local miners in preference to the Davy lamp. The lamp and miners in time became known as 'Geordies'.

Fourth Suggestion

When George Stephenson addressed a Parliamentary Commission "his blunt speech and dialect drew contemptuous sneers". From then on, colliers (boats taking coal from Tyneside to London) and the men who worked on them were called 'Geordies'.

Fifth Suggestion

The term Geordie' was originally a form of abuse first used by local showman Billy Purvis to put down a rival. This was in 1823, when the word was used in this context due to the unpopularity of King George III who became insane.

Emperor Hadrian

Hadrian is believed to be the only bearded Roman Emperor, he never saw his wall completed.

It is estimated that Hadrian's Wall is constructed from 3.7 million tonnes of stone. It is a World Heritage Site.

Valuable Tablets

Writing tablets found at Vindolanda are considered by the British Museum to be the most prized items in their collection.

One of the tablets informs a soldier that clean underwear has been sent.

King Arthur

King Arthur is reputed to have held court at a castle at Sewingshields Craggs close to Hadrian's Wall.

It is widely accepted that King Arthur travelled and defended his kingdom. His life has been subject to 'myth and legend' for hundreds of years.

Royal Palace

King Edwin of Northumbria defeated the West Saxons in 626AD and proclaimed himself the King of all England.

Ad Gefrin near Yeavering Bell in the Cheviots is the site of his Royal Palace. The location was discovered in 1949.

Venerable Bede

Almost all of what is currently known about Anglo-Saxon Britain is due to the work of Jarrow's Venerable Bede.

His method of dating events from Christ's birth Anno Domini, became widely accepted after publication of his history of the English and chronological works.

Saint Cuthbert

Cuthbert was the inspiration behind the Lindisfarne Gospels, he spent much of his life as a hermit.

He had a reputation for working miracles! Appointed Bishop of Hexham, he later resigned the post to become Bishop of Lindisfarne to live a solitary life on Inner Farne. He preferred animals to people.

Queen Victoria

Queen Victoria was asked to pay for her meal at a function in Newcastle, she was not amused.

As a result of this insult, she insisted on having the curtains of the Royal Train drawn when ever she passed through Newcastle.

Outstanding Architecture

Niklaus Pevsner, the distinguished architectural historian, described Newcastle as the best designed Victorian town and large city in England.

Grey Street has been voted the best street in Britain by listeners of Radio 4's Today programme.

Tyneside Flats

The minimum distance between Tyneside flats should be 40 ft at the front and 20 ft at the rear. The frontage has a minimum width of 18 ft and the minimum size of a room is 70 sq ft.

Tyne Bridge

The most commonly used symbol of Tyneside. It is sometimes compared to the Sydney Harbour Bridge. It was opened in 1928, four years before the Sydney Harbour Bridge.

When it opened it was the largest single span bridge in Britain.

Millennium Bridge

The unique tilting design is a world first for Tyneside and is now a famous landmark. Operating like a giant eyelid, turning on pivots on both sides of the river, the 600 metric tonne structure has a headroom of 50 m. The bridge provides a pedestrian and cycle link between Newcastle and Gateshead quayside.

Tyne Pedestrian & Cycle Tunnel

When completed in 1951, the approach escalators with an 85' vertical fall were the longest continuous escalators in the world and the first to permit use by cyclists.

William Fox

Born in South Shields in 1812. He left the region for New Zealand to start a new life on the other side of the world.

He was elected Prime Minister of New Zealand four times.

Thomas Spence

A leading 18th century philosopher and socialist. When he was gathering wild nuts in a wood he was confronted and accused of stealing. He pointed out that squirrels and wild animals were able to gather and eat nuts. If he was not allowed to enjoy 'gifts of nature' his status as a human was less than that of a wild animal.

Mary Astell

A pioneering feminist born in the quayside area of Newcastle, she is considered to be the first published feminist. 'A Serious Proposal To The Ladies' was published in 1694 and 'Some Reflections Upon Marriage' followed in 1700.

Emily Wilding Davison

From Longhorsley, near Morpeth; Emily was a highly active Suffragette and was imprisoned several times where she was force-fed. When she barricaded herself into her cell the prison authorities tried to drown her with a hose-pipe, she later became ill. She died when she jumped in front of the King's horse at the Derby on June 4th, 1913.

Ellen Wilkinson MP

Became MP for Jarrow in 1935 and supported the Jarrow Hunger March in 1936.

Nicknamed 'Red Ellen', she recently and posthumously received an honour of having a beer named after her.

Haltwhistle Kidnapping

When Robert de Pykewell was the vicar of Haltwhistle he had the misfortune of being kidnapped by Scottish raiders who demanded a ransom. The good people of Haltwhistle decided that the Scots could keep their vicar.

Town Moor Slaughter

The 'Newcastle Witch Trial' of 1649 found 27 out of 30 witches guilty; 14 were executed on the Town Moor.

One can only wonder how three defendants managed to prove their innocence?

Tynedale Mayhem

In the Hexham riots of 1761 it is believed that about fifty protesters were killed and hundreds injured when soldiers opened fire on them. It was one of a series of protests against the introduction of balloting to select men for three years military service.

Public Execution

n August 1832 William Jobling was the last man to be publicly gibbeted at Jarrow Slake.

Victorian Immorality

The Chief Constable of Newcastle's 1836 report identified 71 brothels and 46 houses of ill repute. 18 years later in 1854 more than a 100 brothels and 500 public houses and beer shops were identified.

You're Knicked!

The world's first use of a car in a 'police chase' took place in Newcastle on August 15th in 1900. A policeman commandeered a car and its driver to pursue a drunk on a horse. A mile later the drunk was successfully apprehended.

Thomas Addison

Born in Longbenton, he founded endocrinology and was the first person to describe the symptoms of adrenal insufficiency which is now known as Addison's disease.

It was his work at Guy's Hospital that established the institution as a famous medical school.

Sir George Airy

From Alnwick, a geophysicist and astronomer with an impressive list of achievements.

He determined the mass of the earth from gravitational measurements in mines. Airy invented a cylindrical lens for the correction of astigmatism.

He promoted the adoption of Greenwich Mean Time (using Airy's observatory at Grenwich as the starting point, on the line of zero longitude). GMT became Britain's legal time in 1880 when Airy started the practice of sending out time signals by telegraph.

He is sometimes incorrectly credited with discovering Neptune. Airy was, however Astronomer Royal when the planet was discovered.

Neil Bartlett

Neil Bartlett was born in Newcastle. Inert gases were believed to be elements that were unable to form molecules with other elements, he discovered that they could combine with selected other elements and were therefore not absolutely inert.

Arthur Holmes

From Hebburn on Tyne, Arthur developed the dating of rocks and the measurement of radioactive decay in uranium. One of his major achievements was the dating of the earth.

William Turner

The 'Father of English Botany' was born in Morpeth. His *Herbal*, published in three parts, was the first in English containing original material. He identified and named numerous plant species.

Windscreen Wiper

Gladstone Adams, a photographer from Whitley Bay, patented an early windscreen wiper in 1911. A model of his design can be seen at the Discovery Museum in Newcastle. His brother apparently invented the sliding seat used in rowing boats.

Hydraulic Crane

William George Armstrong, born in Newcastle. With the riches from his armaments factory, he bought and refurbished Bamburgh Castle. He invented the hydraulic crane and an innovative side-loading battle gun. He also built Cragside (which was the first house lit by hydroelectricity) and a stately house in Jesmond Dene.

Trilby Hat

Following John James Fenwick's first store at 5 Northumberland Street in 1882, he opened a shop in London in 1891. When there was a stage production of George Du Maurier's 'Trilby', with leading lady Dorothea Baird, John James Fenwick made her a soft felt hat complete with narrow brim and indented crown. This was the first trilby hat.

Control Column (Joy Stick)

Arthur George, a Newcastle motor engineer built aircraft as a hobby. Arthur wanted to overcome the problem of having to use several levers to control each part of an aircraft. He designed a multi-pivoted 'control column' from spare motor parts and patented his invention in 1909.

The term 'joystick' was coined by early aviators who flew in the

First World War. They had difficult cramped conditions so clearly considered it a 'joy' to be able to control many of the aeroplane's functions with one column, conveniently placed between their legs. Or, perhaps there is another reason why early aviators invented the name 'joy stick'.

Fishing Reel

The 'Perfect Fishing Reel' was patented by Forster Hardy in 1888. His design used ball bearings so that the reel was "smooth and fast running", enabling fishermen to cast further. The company that he founded is still making fishing tackle; Alnwick based, House of Hardy.

Flavoured Crisps

The first ever flavoured crisps are believed to have been invented by William Hogget of Whickham, Gateshead, who developed vinegar flavoured crisps.

Light Switch

The electric light switch was invented in 1884 by John Henry Holmes, it was then called the 'quick break' switch as it had the familiar snap off action that is still in use today.

Steam Turbines

Whilst working for Clarke, Chapman and Co., Charles Parsons developed the steam turbine. He went on to design and make Turbinia, the world's first steam turbine ship and at the time, the world's fastest ship. Other innovations include: more efficient screw propellers, searchlights and optical systems.

Light Bulb

The incandescent light bulb was invented by Joseph Wilson Swan which he demonstrated at the 'Lit. and Phil.' in Newcastle. A manufacturing plant was set up in Benwell.

Swan was also responsible for the development of the dry photographic process which enabled photography to be enjoyed by 'the masses' as it was no longer necessary to have a laboratory to take and process photographs. The photographic technology developed by Swan is the principle behind photographic film. He also invented a system of duplication (bromide photography) which has been universally used until recently being replaced by digital technology.

Reinforced Concrete

Newcastle based William Boutland Wilkinson invented reinforced concrete and was known to be using the technique as early as 1854.

He did not take out a patent for his invention which 'paved' the way for Frenchman Joseph Monier to do so in 1867.

Kippers

Kippers are believed to have been invented by John Woodger, in Seahouses, by accident in 1843. He left herring on a rack overnight over a burning fire. At first he thought that the fish would have been ruined, he discovered that the fish were wonderful!

Self-Righting Lifeboat

There is dispute about who invented the first self-righting lifeboat. In a competition to design and build a lifeboat, William Woodhave's designs were incorporated into a model submitted by Henry Greathead and accepted by the competition committee. Who designed the first lifeboat, Greathead or Woodhave?

The first purpose-built lifeboat in the world was the 'Original' launched at South Shields.

The first volunteer life brigade was formed at Tynemouth in 1864.

Grace Darling

She lived with her father on the Longstone Lighthouse. On September 7th, 1838 she rescued nine sailors from the steamship Forfarshire which was sailing from Hull to Dundee.

Grace became a national heroine, sadly she died four years later in 1842.

Coal

Wallsend Coal was the generic term given to the premium grade of house coal. Customers who wished to order the highest grade coal continued requesting 'Wallsend Coal' long after it ceased to be mined in Wallsend.

Buckingham Palace used to source coal from Shilbottle Colliery, near Alnwick.

Coal attracted a range of industries to locate in the region in the 18th and 19th centuries.

Glass manufacturers needed coal to power their furnaces and so Tyneside became a centre for glass making.

The demand for rope in mines and shipbuilding led to the development of a vibrant rope manufacturing industry along both banks of the Tyne.

Ships

The Mauritania built by Swan Hunter in 1906 held the Blue Ribbon award for the fastest crossing of the Atlantic for 22 years.

The largest vessel to sail up the Tyne was the Bonga in 2002. It weighs 30,000 tonnes which is equivalent to 30,000 double-decker buses.

Coble

The only surviving indigenous craft of the north-east coast, designed to be launched off open beaches. Their method of construction has similarities to that of Viking longships, they are built by bending steamed planks over lightweight frames. They are between 25 ft and 35 ft long with a beam of 7 ft to 9 ft. Fewer than 200 survive.

Keel Boat

Up to 50 ft long they sailed from harbours and rivers all along the coast. They disappeared about a hundred years ago when they were made redundant by modern boats.

A few Keel boats can be seen cut in half, upturned and used huts on Holy Island.

Tyne Keel

A barge used by Keelmen to transport coal on to colliers to the harbour. They had a key role in the development of the coal industry.

Keelmen used to race along the Tyne competing for work.

George Stephenson

Considered to be the most important figure in the development of the railway.

The standard gauge which is used by 60% of the world is credited to George Stephenson. One story is that he took an average of cart axle widths when deciding on a gauge of 4 ft 8 $\frac{1}{2}$ inches.

Robert Stephenson

Worked with his father on railway projects and became manager of his father's engine works.

His most visible legacy is the High Level Bridge over the Tyne and the Royal Border Bridge in Berwick upon Tweed.

He is buried in Westminster Cathedral.

Tanfield Railway

Considered by railway enthusiasts to the be world's oldest railway.

It was built in 1725 to carry coal to Dunston.

It is now partly preserved with a large collection of Tyneside-built locomotives.

Felling Metro Station

Opposite Felling Metro Station is a small stone building beside the B.R. line; this is the original Felling Station and possibly the oldest surviving unaltered railway station in the world.

Be-Ro Flour

Self-raising flour was invented by Thomas Bell of Longhorsley. The name is a combination of BE (ll) and RO (al).

Many generations have learned how to bake with the **Be-Ro** promotional cookbook.

Domestos

nvented in the Ouseburn area of Newcastle by Wilfred and Ivy Handley in 1929.

They also pioneered the use of soft plastic bottles that could be squeezed for washing-up liquid.

Earl Grey Tea

The world's most popular blend of tea. It was sent as a gift to Prime Minister Earl Grey, after an envoy on a diplomatic mission saved the life of a Chinese Mandarin. Oil of bergamot gives the tea its unique flavour. Earl Grey loved the aroma and flavour so much he asked Twinings to reproduce the blend.

Lucozade

Invented by a Newcastle pharmacist to build up the blood sugar level in children, following concern about poor diet and health.

Fairy Soap

World-famous Fairy Soap was originally a Thomas Hedley and Co. product.

The company was bought by Proctor and Gamble in the 1930s.

Greggs

Originally a family bakery business founded by John Gregg on Tyneside in 1930.

The company now has stores all over Britain. Its store at Newcastle Airport is probably the only outlet selling food at high-street prices.

Malling Pottery

Founded in Sunderland in 1762, the company moved to Newcastle in 1817 and became the biggest pottery in the world! Production ceased in 1963, the site is now Hoults Estate (formerly Hoults Removals).

Newcastle Brown Ale

The recipe for the beer that once could only be brewed in Newcastle was developed by Colonel James Herbert Porter in 1927.

It is now brewed in Gateshead at the Federation Brewery.

Bedlington Terriers

A famous breed of dog, originally known as the Rothberg Terrier. John Ainsley from Bedlington owned the first dog recognised and called a Bedlington Terrier.

One story is that Bedlington Terriers are developed from a breed of dogs used by gypsies in the Rothbury area.

Cheviot Sheep

Wild goats have roamed the Cheviots for over 200 years. They are descended from domesticated goats.

In the summer they roam the tops of the hills, in winter months they are forced down to the valley bottoms.

Chillingham Cattle

A unique breed, they have been isolated since 1270 when Chillingham Park was enclosed. The herd ranges in size between forty and sixty animals.

Cuddy Duck

The eider duck is an icon of Northumberland, it has been given the nickname 'cuddy duck' after St. Cuthbert.

Grey Seals

Large numbers of grey seals can be seen around the Farne Islands. Breeding takes place in October, when territorial fights and skirmishes take place. More often than not the wounds are superficial.

Red Kites

Recently reintroduced to suburban Gateshead, they can be seen soaring high in the skies above the Metro Centre.

Red Squirrels

Northumberland is the last county in England where the red squirrel has a stronghold in the wild.

Whitelee Moor

At 1,500 hectares, Whitelee Moor is the largest National Nature Reserve in England.

Located adjacent to the Scottish Borders with magnificent views of the Cheviot and across moorland.

Tenantry Column-Alnwick

Built in 1815 with a subscription from a thousand of the 4th Duke of Northumberland's tenants after he lowered rents by 25% during a period of agricultural depression.

Unfortunately the rent was raised soon after the column was built and it became known as the 'farmers folly'.

Stan Laurel-North Shields

Stan Laurel lived some of his early life in North Shields.

It is believed that the inspiration behind the Laurel and Hardy film, where they move a piano up a flight of steps was gained after Stan watched a North Shields family move their household goods up the steps from the fish quay.

The Angel of the North

Designed by Antony Gormley, in just a few years this symbol of the gateway to Tyneside has become a national icon.

It is seen by 90,000 people every day.

Earl Grey-Newcastle

The sculpture is by Edward Hughes Bailey, who is also responsible for Nelson on Nelson's Column.

Earl Grey not only had a blend of tea named after him, he is also one of the greatest parliamentarians ever.

The Old Gaol, Hexham

The first purpose-built gaol in England was built in 1330 to imprison convicted Reivers.

It now houses an exhibition on Reiving.

Hoppings

Held every June on the Town Moor in Newcastle. Set up by the Temperance movement to demonstrate that people can enjoy themselves without the need to drink alcohol.

Traditionally everyone gets soaked, as it usually rains.

Newcastle Beer Festival

Celebrating its 30th birthday in 2006, the Newcastle Beer Festival is the region's biggest annual indoor party.

It is organised by the Tyneside and Northumberland branch of the Campaign for Real Ale.

Bainbridges

Thought to be the oldest department store in the world.

The exact date it opened is not known, but it is believed to have been during 1838.

Metrocentre

Gateshead's Metrocentre is the biggest out of town shopping complex in Europe and the first out of town shopping complex in the U.K.

Dog Show

The Kennel Club's first dog show was held at Newcastle Town Hall in 1859. It is believed to be the world's first dog show. There were sixty entries of pointers and setters.

What about Redheads?

Britain's first beauty contest was staged at the Olympia Theatre, Newcastle in 1905. The 'Blonde and Brunette Beauty Show' was open to all young ladies over the age of sixteen.

Street Lighting

osely Street, Newcastle, in 1811 became the first street to have gas lighting and in 1880 became the first street to be lit by electricity.

Baby

Marian Chambers was the world's smallest baby. Born in South Shields in 1938, she weighed only ten ounces, she died aged 44.

Her life is celebrated at South Shields Museum.

Kielder

I t is the largest forest in England and one of the largest man-made forests in Europe with 150 million standing trees.

Kielder Water is the largest man-made reservoir in Europe. It is seven miles long and holds a volume of water that would enable everyone in the world to flush the toilet simultaneously and meet demand.

Motion Simulator Ride

The longest motion simulator ride in the world is at LIFE Interactive World.

Wind Tunnel Testing

The world's largest wind turbine blade test facility is based at NaRec in Blyth. Tyneside and Northumberland is a leading centre for the development of alternative energy generation techniques.

Longest Place Names

Blakehopeburnhaugh and Cottonhopeburnfoot in Northumberland are the longest official place names in England.

Blake means black, hope is a side valley, burn is a stream and haugh is a strip of pasture along a valley. Cottonhopeburnfoot is the place where the Cotton meets the Rede.

Britain's Oldest Dwelling

Howick located on the Northumberland coast is believed to be the oldest dwelling in the Britain. Constructed around 7,800 B.C., discovered by amateur archeologists John Davies and Jim Hutchinson, it has since been excavated by Newcastle University. It is one of the few stone age dwellings in Britain.

Read All About It

The South Shields Gazette is the UK's oldest provincial evening paper.

Team Valley Trading Estate

The first government sponsored trading estate in the world.

It was built in the mid-thirties to combat unemployment caused by the great depression. The boundaries were expanded in 1951 and it has continued to grow.

The Toon

Current players are excluded as it is hoped that their tally will grow with every match played. Alan Shearer should soon occupy the top spot.

<u>Most League & Cup Appearances</u>
496 Jimmy Lawrence 1904-1922
472 Frank Hudspeth 1910-1929
457 Frank Clark 1962-1975
432 Bill McCracken 1904-1923
431 Alf McMichael 1949-1963

Most League & Cup Goals

Players who have scored more than a hundred goals.

200 Jackie Milburn 1946-57

153 Len White 1946-57

143 Hughie Gallacher 1925-30

121 Malcolom McDonald 1971-76

119 Peter Beardsley 1983-97

113 Bobby Mitchell 1949-61

113 Tom McDonald 1921-31

101 Neil Harris 1920-25

Beowulf

The first major poem written in a European vernacular language, originated in Northumbria in the 7th or early 8th century. It is about events that took place in the 6th century, it did not appear in print until 1815.

Basil Bunting

The first and principal British modernist poet was born at 258 Denton Road in what was then Scotswood-on-Tyne. His 1966 work 'Briggflats' celebrates Northumberland.

Robinson Crusoe

Daniel Defoe apparently wrote the classic story based on the experiences of Alexander Selkirk whilst he was living in Gateshead. It is one of the most translated books in the history of literature.

Anti-utopia

Yeugeni Zamyatin a Russian working on Tyneside wrote 'We' the first anti-utopia, based on his experiences in shipyards. The book is considered to be an influence on Aldous Huxley's 'Brave New World' and George Orwell's '1984'.

Historic Drama

Catherine Cookson is a publishing phenomenon; an international best seller and for many years the most borrowed author from libraries.

Born in Jarrow, she has received an accolade from South Tyneside which markets itself as 'Cookson Country'. Whilst our most prolific author is no longer with us, her stories live on.

Ten Great Television Series

<u>Television series set in the region</u>

Auf Wiedersehen, Pet

Badger

Byker Grove

Crocodile Shoes

55^0 North

The Likely Lads

Our Friends In The North

Spender

Supergran

When The Boat Comes In

Great Films

Many great films have been made in the region.

Alien III

Becket

El Cid

Get Carter

Harry Potter series

Macbeth

Mary Queen of Scots

Purely Belta

Robin Hood Prince of Thieves

Traditional Music

Northumberland is the only county in Britain that has an instrument named after it. The Northumbrian Pipes are more closely related to French small pipes than bagpipes. It is probably due to Northumbrian Pipes that Northumberland has an unbroken musical tradition.

Rock and Roll

The Shadows are considered by many to be Britain's best ever rock and roll band. It was formed by two lads from Newcastle: Hank Marvin and Bruce Welch.

Folk-rockers

Lindisfarne have enjoyed huge commercial and critical success.

Their Christmas concerts were a legend. Their 1971 'Fog On The Tyne' was the year's best selling album. After the sad death of Alan Hull, the band were never the same again. They retired gracefully in autumn 2003.

Stottie Bread

A stottie is described by the 'Flour Advisory Bureau' as: "A large round bap from the north-east of England. The Geordie stottie has a fluffy texture."

Stotties can be wholemeal, white, granary, or indeed how ever you prefer your bread. The traditional stottie filling is ham and pease pudding.

General Guidance for Stotties

1 Use a standard bread dough recipe or recipe of your choice.

2 Use a baking tray instead of a loaf tin.

3 Bake as a huge bun (following the cooking time for the dough mix), they should be between 1 and 2 inches thick.

Leek Pudding

A form of suet pudding often served with stew.

Ingredients

100 gm self-raising flour

50 gm suet

1 leek

A pinch of salt

Method

1 Mix flour, suet and add a pinch of salt.

2 Roll out the pastry.

3 Chop/slice the leek.

4 Put the leek inside the pastry and roll up.

5 Place in cloth, or wrap in foil.

6 Immerse in boiling water and boil for about two hours.

Admiral Collingwood

When Nelson was killed Admiral Cuthbert Collingwood took over control of the British navy and won the Battle of Trafalgar in 1805. This victory ended Napoleon's hopes of invading Britain.

Richard Annand

Second Lieutenant Annand of South Shields won the Victoria Cross in the Second World War. He was presented with his medal by King George VI, after fighting off a German attack of a bridge by running forward over open ground with hand grenades. He also saved the life of an injured batman by using a wheelbarrow to rescue him through open land.

Northumberland Flag

Based on a traditional flag which is possibly the oldest flag design in Britain. The Venerable Bede records a banner of purple and gold hung over the tomb of St. Oswald. The flag of the ancient Kingdom has eight alternate stripes of red and yellow/gold.

Northumberland Tartan

Known as the Shepherd Tartan in Scotland, the Northumberland Tartan dates back to Roman Times. A scrap of black and white check was found in a Roman bottle and is the oldest check fabric ever found.

The black and white check tartan has been used by the Duke of Northumberland since the 18th century.

Northumberland Flower

A wild geranium bloody crane's-bill (Geranium Sanguineum) was voted county flower for Northumberland in 2002, when Plantlife International launched their county flower campaign.

County of Castles

Northumberland has more castles open to the public than any other county in Britain.

Newcastle Disease

A disease that only effects poultry. It is a virus that is marked by the loss of egg production in older birds and causes paralysis in chicks.

Newcastle Glass

A type of goblet credited to the Beilby family who created the design during the 1770s and 1780s. Glass-makers across Europe copied the style which then became known as 'Newcastle glass'.

River Tyne

For many years the Tyne was a heavily polluted, dirty river. It is now the best river in Britain to catch salmon. Fishing for trout has also become popular, attracting visitors from all over Britain and beyond.

Coming and Going

Newcastle Airport is the fastest growing provincial airport in Britain. There are scheduled flights to places all over Europe and in 2006 scheduled flights start to New York.

Arts and Culture

For many generations Tyneside and Northumberland was associated with coal, shipbuilding and heavy industry. Over recent years it has captured national and international attention through arts and culture; Alnwick Garden, Angel of the North, The Baltic, Centre for the Children's Book and The Sage have all helped to change the region's image.